Baby Book

MAY ALL BABES BE BROUGHT INTO THIS WORLD WITH LOVE, SO THAT THEY MAY BABY IT ON.

Baby Book

This book belongs to:
Max N.

Illustrated by Robyn Phillips

The Five Mile Press

The Five Mile Press Pty Ltd
415 Jackson St, San Francisco
CA, 94111, USA
www.fivemile.com.au
Designed by Robyn Phillips

This edition first published 2008
Reprinted 2009

Printed in China

Contents

Family Tree

Grandfather

_____

Grandmother

_____

Father

_____

Brothers

_____

_____

_____

Grandfather

_____

Grandmother

_____

Mother

_____

Sisters

_____

_____

_____

Baby

_____

Baby's Arrival

Date and time of birth

_____

Weight

_____

Length

_____

Circumference of head

_____

Color of eyes

_____

Color of hair

_____

Father present?

_____

Baby was early/late

_____

Blood group

_____

Birthmarks

_____

Place of birth

_____

Doctor's name

_____

Who does baby resemble?

_____

Monday's child is fair of face.
Tuesday's child is full of grace.
Wednesday's child is full of woe.
Thursday's child has far to go.
Friday's child is loving and giving
Saturday's child works hard for a living
And the child that is born on the Sabbath day
Is fair and wise and good and gay.

Dear little baby born so small
One day you'll grow to stand so tall
We'll love you when you're big
We love you whilst you're small
Infact little baby, there'll not be a day
When we don't love you at all.

9

Visitors

Visitors

Gifts and cards

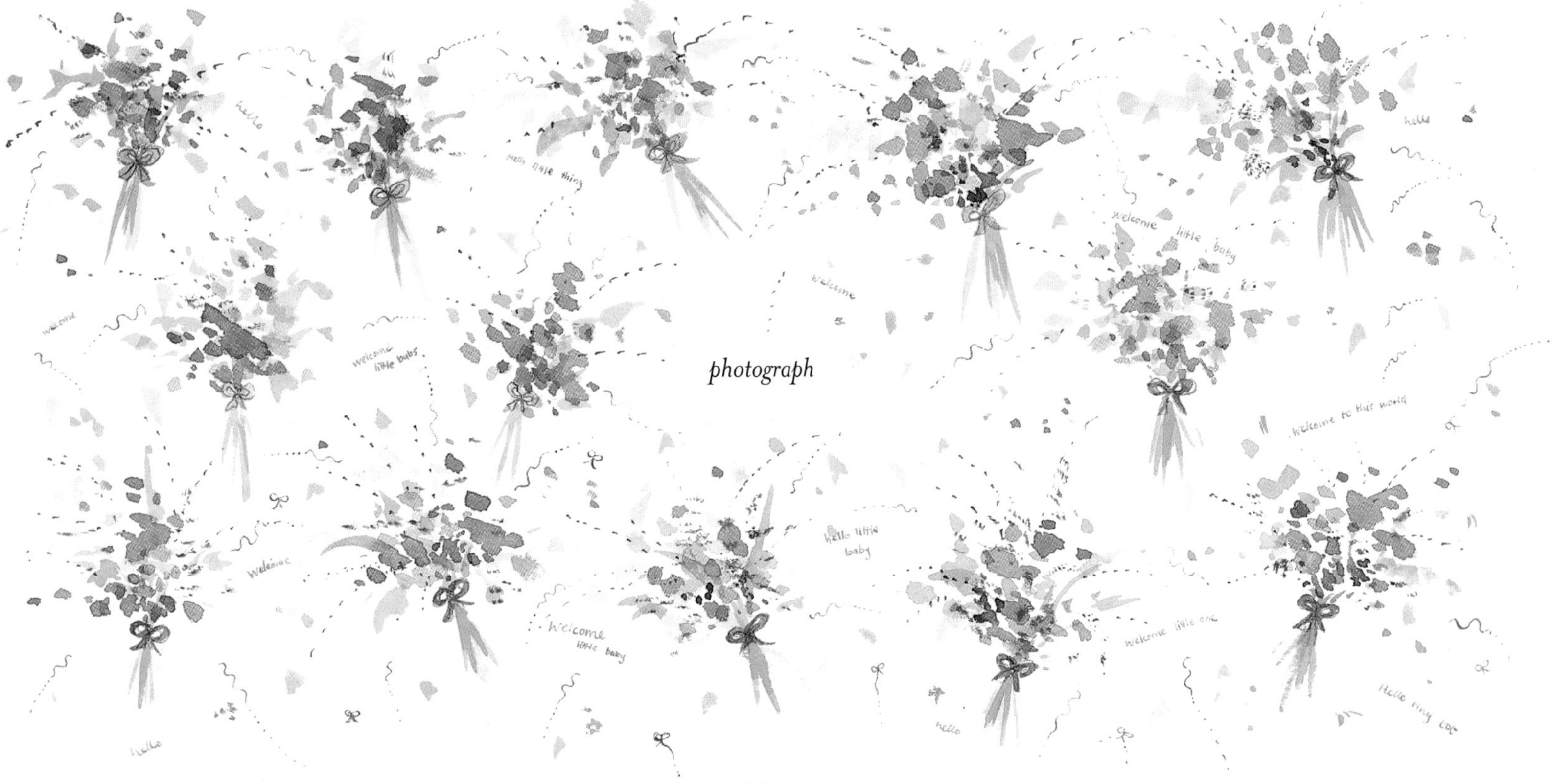

_____

_____

_____

_____

_____

_____

_____

_____

_____

_____

_____

_____

_____

_____

photograph

First Days

Baby is home and the family is complete. This is an exciting but tiring time. Don't be too house-proud, enjoy your baby. Try to organize someone to help you with the chores so that you can get the most out of these early and important days.

Baby's feeding times

_____

Duration of each feed

_____

Breast or bottle

_____

Sleeping times

_____

Preferred sleeping position

_____

Wakeful times

_____

Does baby eat and sleep well?

_____

Coming home date

_____

Who was there to welcome the baby

_____

_____

Baby's Development

During the first six months of life you will see your baby's personality grow and develop. That first smile, the realization that your baby recognizes you, when those little hands first reach for a loved toy — all these moments are precious and worth recording.

Baby first focuses

_____

Baby's first smile

_____

Baby first sucks thumb or dummy

_____

Baby first discovers hands

_____

Baby first discovers feet

_____

Baby first reaches for an object

_____

Baby first says da-da

_____

Baby first says ma-ma

_____

Baby first claps hands

_____

Baby first drinks from a cup

_____

photograph

Sounds

Most mothers can recognize their own baby's cry in a room full of crying infants. That's because, even without words, your baby can communicate a great deal. As baby develops, so does the range of emotions and messages that can be conveyed.

Baby recognizes mother's voice

_____

Baby recognizes father's voice

_____

First giggle

_____

First gurgle (around 4-6 weeks)

_____

First oohs, ees, and aahs

_____

First squeal of delight

_____

First sounds using lips (ba-ba, ma-ma, pa-pa)

_____

First animal noise

_____

First word

_____

First recognizes own name

_____

First recognizes simple instructions

_____

First says no!

_____

Playtime

This little piggy went to market, This little piggy stayed home, This little piggy had roast beef, And this little piggy had none, And this little piggy went wee wee wee wee wee wee wee wee wee...

Dance little baby, dance up high
Never mind baby, mother is by
Up to the ceiling, down to the ground.
Backwards + forwards, round and round.

Round and round the garden like a teddy bear, One step, two step, and tickle you under there.

Your baby's favorite toys

_____

Your baby's favorite games

_____

Your baby's favorite songs, lullabies

_____

Your baby's favorite stories

_____

The Christening

A name is probably the only thing that is given to a baby that remains for a lifetime. Sometimes there are family names that are passed through generations; often parents spend many months thinking of a suitable name. Whatever the outcome, it is good to celebrate the final decision!

Baby's name

_____

Names of godparents

_____

Ceremony was held at

_____

Baby was named by (eg minister)

_____

How your baby reacted

_____

What baby wore

_____

Who was present

_____

Where you celebrated afterwards

_____

Gifts

_____

photograph

Getting Around

A baby simply cannot move very much in the early weeks of life, so always seems to be out of danger. But soon enough, baby learns to roll over ... crawl ... and discovers that getting around is fun! Now mother has to be in all places at once!

Baby can hold head up

_____

Baby can sit with help

_____

Sits alone

_____

Rolls on to back

_____

Rolls right over

_____

Jack and Jill went up the hill
To fetch a pail of water;
Jack fell down and broke his crown,
And Jill came tumbling after.

First crawls

First trip in the car

First goes shopping in pram

First outing in stroller

Bathtime

Bathtime is a good opportunity to introduce a different game – splashing! Babies usually love being in warm water and the relaxing and calming effects are just what is needed before bedtime.

First enjoys bath

_____

First time in a big bath

_____

First bubble bath

_____

Favorite bath toys

_____

First swim

_____

First time in the sea

_____

First plays under the sprinkler

_____

photograph

photograph

Bedtime

Your baby's sleep pattern: newborn

_____

First unbroken night

_____

Your baby's sleep pattern: at 6 months

_____

Your baby's sleep pattern: at 18 months

_____

Favorite soft toy

_____

First time in a crib

_____

First time in a bed

_____

First babysitter

_____

Sleep, baby, sleep:
Sweet baby, go to sleep
Too sweet for words, how could you tell
How sweet my baby is —
More than the trees on every hill,
More than every blade of grass,
More than all the stars in the sky
More than all the rice stalks in the field?
This babe asleep
Is more, more sweet
Than all of these.

photograph

Teething

A baby can feel discomfort when cutting teeth. Often it helps to give baby a rusk or a teething ring to relieve the sensation felt on the gums. Eventually your baby will have twenty 'milk teeth' and the first of these may begin to appear at any time from birth to twelve months.

First tooth_____

Second tooth_____

Third tooth_____

Fourth tooth_____

Fifth tooth_____

Sixth tooth_____

Seventh tooth_____

Eighth tooth_____

Ninth tooth_____

Tenth tooth_____

Eleventh tooth_____

Twelfth tooth_____

Thirteenth tooth_____

Fourteenth tooth_____

Fifteenth tooth_____

Sixteenth tooth_____

Seventeenth tooth_____

Eighteenth tooth_____

Nineteenth tooth_____

Twentieth tooth_____

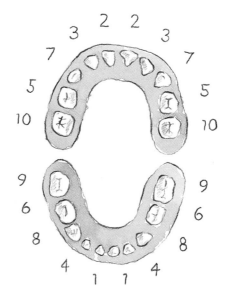

1. Lower front teeth (around 6-8 months)
2. Upper front teeth (around 7-9 months)
3. Upper side teeth (around 8-9 months)
4. Lower side teeth (around 9-10 months)
5. Upper first molars (around 12 months)
6. Lower first molars (around 14 months)
7. Upper eye teeth (around 16 months)
8. Lower eye teeth (around 18 months)
9. Lower second molars (around 22-24 months)
10. Upper second molars (around 24-26 months)

Eating

After months of living on milk alone, the exciting day arrives when your baby can taste 'solids' for the first time. Even just a teaspoon of baby rice is a totally new experience. In the following weeks it's good to try a range of simple taste sensations, such as mashed bananas and stewed apples.

First solid food

_____

Weaned from bottle/breast

_____

First drink from cup with help

_____

First drink from cup without help

_____

Favorite solid food

_____

Favorite drink

_____

First Steps

Among the many stages of development in a baby's life, learning to walk is often considered to be the biggest milestone. All of a sudden your baby is transformed to a toddler and nothing within reach is safe!

Baby first stands when held

Baby opens a door

Baby first stands while held by the hands

Baby first climbs out of the crib

Baby first clambers into a standing position

Baby first climbs out of the stroller

Baby takes first steps held by the hands

Your baby takes first step alone

Baby first gets up on to a chair

Baby walks!

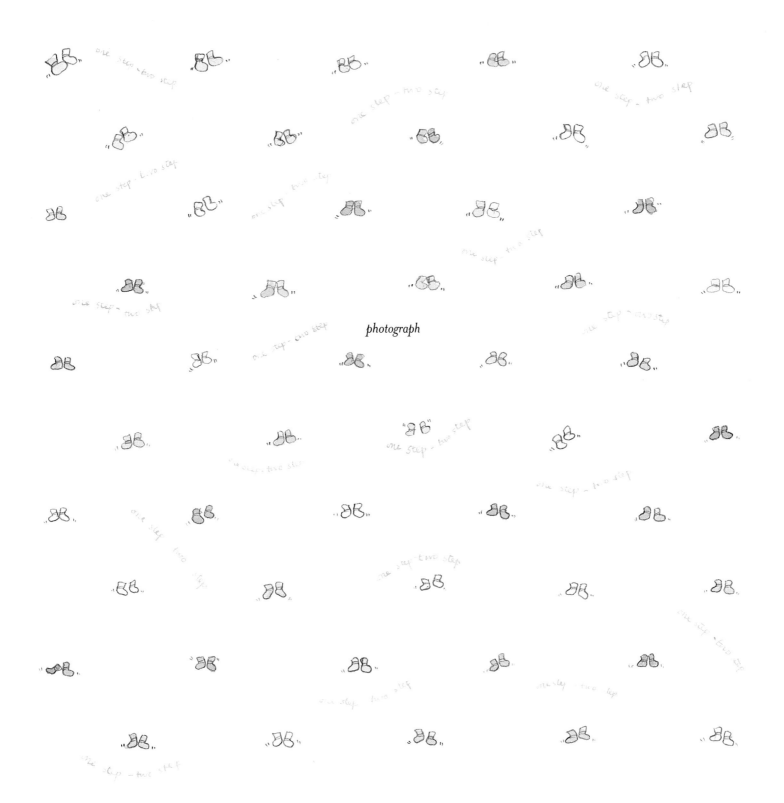

photograph

First Birthday

Baby's first birthday present

_____

Did baby enjoy the party?

_____

How the birthday was celebrated

_____

Who was there?

_____

Everything's been different
All the day long
Lovely things have happened
Nothing has gone wrong

Nobody has scolded me,
Everyone has smiled.
Isn't it delicious
to be a birthday child?

photograph

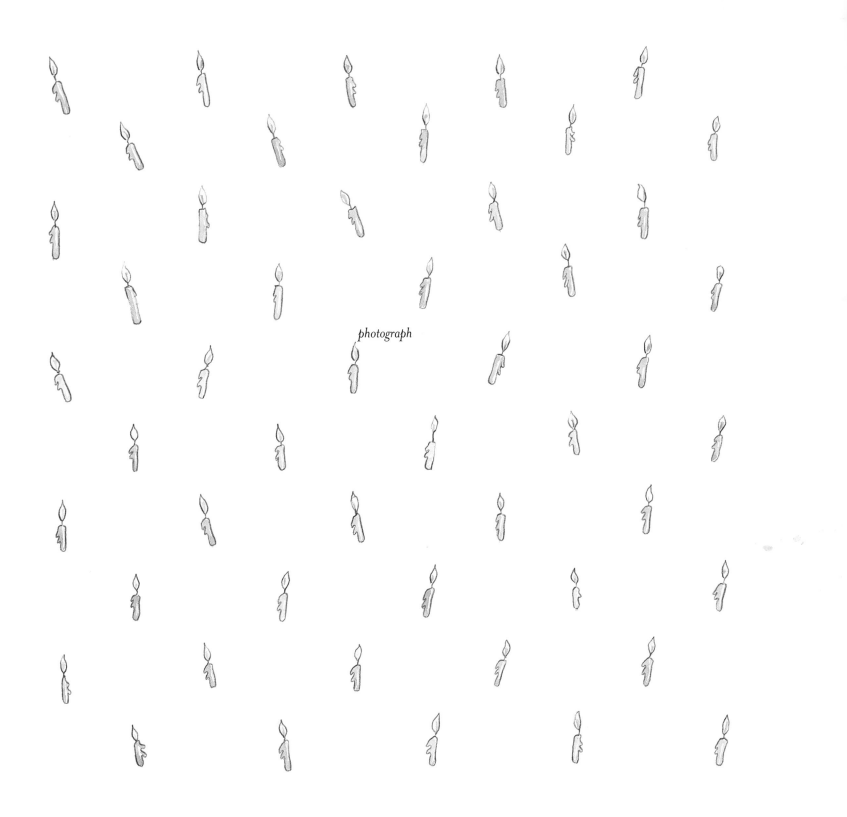

photograph

First Christmas

Christmas is a great time for families to get together and all the fuss of preparations, noise, and excitement make a very stimulating experience for a young baby. Notice how baby heads for the brightly colored wrapping paper on the presents under the tree!

Little Jack Horner sat in a corner
Eating his Christmas pie
He put in his thumb
And pulled out a plum
And said, "What a good boy am I!"

How your baby celebrated the first Christmas

_____

Where you spent Christmas

_____

Who else was there?

_____

Baby's first Christmas present

_____

Baby's favorite present

_____

photograph

photograph

First Twelve Months

Even though you may tire of constantly purchasing new clothes for your baby, you undoubtedly take great pleasure in seeing all the rapid developments occurring.

Most babies treble their birthweight in the first year of life but this rate of growth does slow down in the following years.

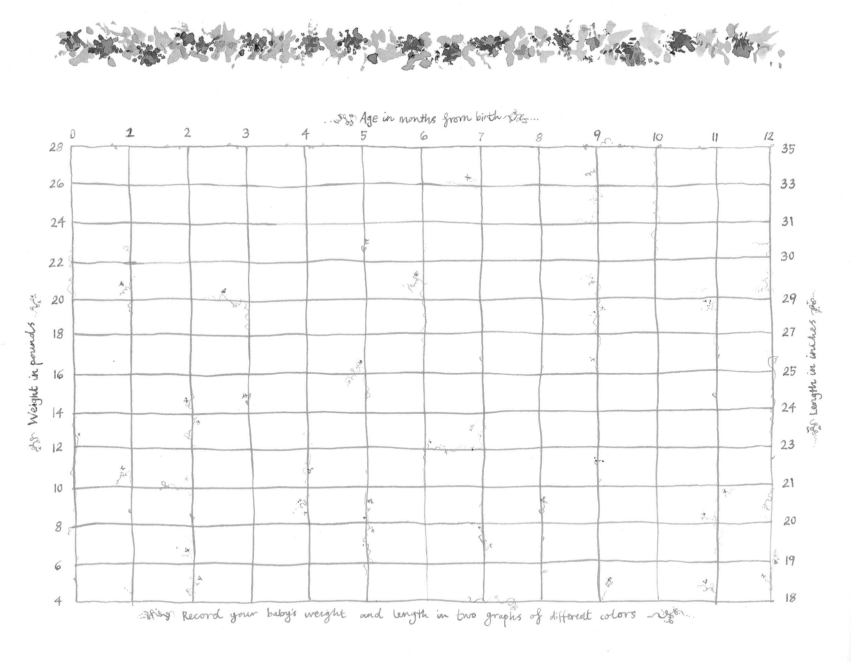

Age in months from birth

Weight in pounds

Length in inches

Record your baby's weight and length in two graphs of different colors

32

To remind yourself of just how tiny your newborn baby was, it is a good idea to make an impression of the hand and foot prints.

Simply press your baby's hand against a dye stamp pad and then press the hand gently in the space below. Repeat for the foot. (It is easy to remove the ink from baby's hand and foot.)

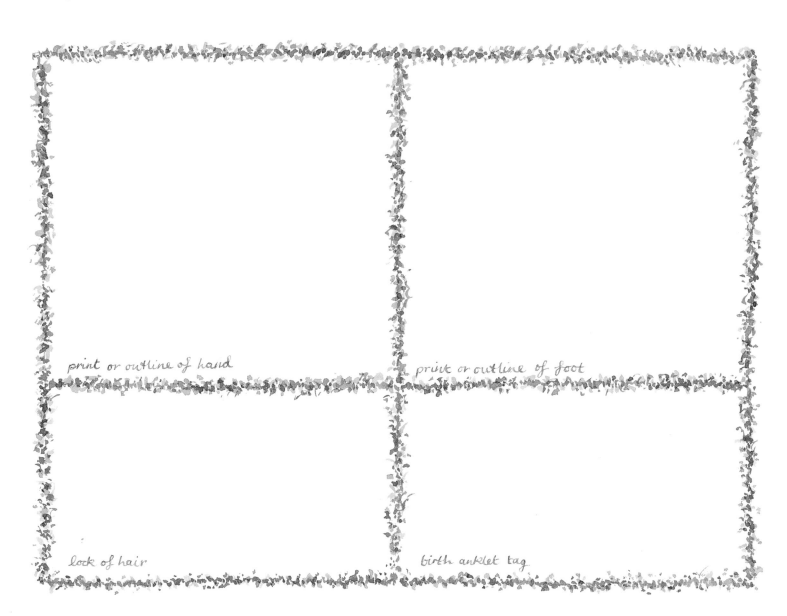

print or outline of hand

print or outline of foot

lock of hair

birth anklet tag

Memories

When you reflect on the first twelve months of your baby's
life, there will be many situations that stir the emotions.
Think of the time when you first went on a picnic and your
baby saw the ducks on the pond – or you brought home a
new kitten – or there was a special family celebration. All
are memories that are a joy to capture.

Memorable moments

_____ _____

_____ _____

_____ _____

_____ _____

_____ _____

_____ _____

_____ _____

_____ _____

photograph

35

Baby's Favorite Things

Favorite toys

_____

Animals

_____

Clothes

_____

Friends

_____

Stories

_____

Games

_____

Songs

_____

Foods

_____

photograph

Getting into Trouble

Sometimes a child's idea of having fun does not measure up to yours! Experimenting with your lipstick and painting the wall may be an imitation of what you do, but the result is hardly the same when your baby has a go!

First drew on a wall

_____

First attempt at illustrating books

_____

First tries to help with shopping

_____

First tried to wash up

_____

First made the bed or other activities

_____

_____

_____

_____

Pet Hates

It is surprising how soon a baby's personality shines through and how easy it is to know when your baby does not like something. Unfortunately, not all toys and food are a hit and it's just by trial and error that you find out your baby's dislikes.

Least favorite toys

_____

Animals

_____

Clothes

_____

Stories

_____

Games

_____

Songs/rhymes

_____

Foods

_____

Other pet hates

_____

First Holidays

Taking a baby along on a holiday requires much more planning and organization than ever before. Although that first holiday away with your baby can be fraught with unforeseen problems, there will certainly be a lot of fun and surprises.

Date of first holiday

_____

Where you went

_____

Who went with you

_____

First paddle

_____

First swim

_____

First sandcastle

_____

First ice cream

_____

little shells

tiny shells

tiny shells

photograph

tiny shells

little shells

tiny shells

little shells

little shells

little shells

Medical Records

Vaccinations:

Triple Antigen: diphtheria, tetanus, whooping cough (DTP)
1st dose (approx. 2 months)

_____

Triple Antigen: 2nd dose (approx. 4 months)

_____

Triple Antigen: 3rd dose (approx. 6 months)

_____

Sabin (oral polio): 1st dose (given at same time as Triple
Antigen – approx. 2 months)

_____

Sabin: 2nd dose (approx. 4 months)

_____

Sabin: 3rd dose (approx. 6 months)
Measles/Mumps: (12-15 months)

_____

Triple Antigen (DTP) Booster: 18 months

_____

Common diseases:

Chicken-pox

_____

German measles

_____

Measles

_____

Mumps

_____

Whooping cough

_____

Allergies

_____

Eyesight test

_____

Blood group

_____

The Future

Does your daughter want to be a fireman? Or your son a ballet dancer? Nowadays children can aspire to any profession — the world is open to them. What do you think your little one is likely to be? Try sketching your vision of this wonderful little creature in 20 years' time.

My baby's future

_____   _____

_____   _____

_____   _____

photograph

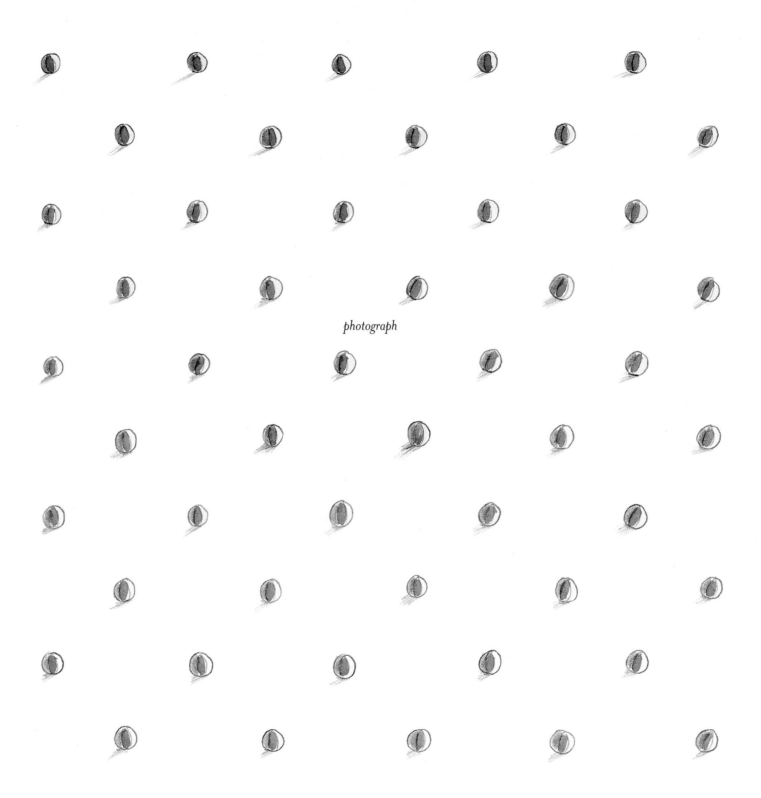

photograph

photograph

photograph